EVERY DAY
Living Poetically

Poetry By
Deborah Baptiste Lee

Every Day
Living Poetically

Poems by
Deborah Baptiste Lee

dlee Dragonfly Publishing

Book Design and digital illustrations
By Patty Atcheson-Melton

ISBN: 978-0-9858839-0-4

Dedication

I dedicate my first book of poetry to
my daughter Kimberlee; my son Christopher
My step-sons Chandler and Jacob
Grandchildren, Paris, Preston, Xander and Annelise
Daughter-in-law Nichole, Son-in-law Raymond, Jessica
and husband, Thomas E. Lee

Acknowledgements

To my Mother, Annette Baptiste
Your creativity has inspired me throughout my life.
Thank you for the next project already in the works.
I am so happy to be co- creating the next book
of children's poetry with you.
I love you mom, You are so talented.
Believe in yourself always.

To Patty Melton
You are so talented. Thank you for encouraging me every
single step of the way. YOU are the reason this book came
together. My heart is full and I will be forever grateful.
I am so blessed to call you my friend.

Table of Contents

Every Day

Everyday I want to meditate
Make time just for me
Open my mind   Clear to find
Pure potentiality

Everyday I want to exercise
Make time just for me
Build and tone   and strengthen bone
More flexibility

Everyday I want to play outside
Make time just for me
Bubbles of soap   Jumping rope
Or swinging joyfully

Everyday I want to learn something new
Make time just for me
Become aware   This knowledge share
With my friends and family

Everyday I want to eat right
Make meals not just for me
That taste so good   I really would
Embrace longevity

Everyday I want to go somewhere
Alone or with a friend
Near or far   By foot or car
The place would just depend

Everyday I want to feel complete
And know I've done my best
Then let it go   And let love flow
I am forever blessed.

ASK
BELIEVE
RECEIVE

The Gift

They've told us through the ages
And let there be no doubt
It has everything to do with
What you think about
You've heard, "Ask it shall be given"
How much simpler does it get
But it takes a little practice
So you don't end in regret.
Thinking
Can get strenuous
So don't forget to breathe.
Go into the silent space

ASK   BELIEVE   RECEIVE

Believe me when I tell you
You are what you think about.
Our thoughts are like a magnet
Don't second guess or doubt.
Pay attention where your thoughts go
What feelings they create.
Therein lies the power
Of what we know as fate.
This gift never places judgment
It's so perfect in design.
Understanding how to use it
May not have crossed your mind.
Dwelling on the negative won't get you very far
Remember how the gift works
It got you where you are.
There's no better way to do it
Than being in the NOW
Awaken your life purpose
The gift will show you how.
Start by being grateful
For everything you have
Focus on abundance
Instead of thinking lack.
Shed the heavy burden of judgment and disdain
It's a lack of self-acceptance
And a source of stress and strain.
Accept this moment as it is
Being present makes the space
For larger life to happen
In a simple state of grace.

Seed upon the wind

Try to block out everything
Except the open sky
Bluer than blue
My favorite hue
Just see what passes by
A bird   A plane   A seagull
A seed upon the wind
Wonder where it's going
Wonder where it's been
Where will the seed take cover
In the ground below
In a lot
Or planters pot
Or will it meet the snow
Maybe in the mountains
Somewhere far away
Maybe it won't touch the ground
Just go in circles round and round
And next year when I'm here again
I'll see the seed and wonder when.

Good Morning

It's chilly today. A nip in the breeze
The leaves are all turning
Falling off of the trees
Red, yellow and scarlet
The sky is light blue
Autumn clouds whisper, "winter's coming, it's true."
Morning is quiet. Even dog doesn't stir
Bunny was eating, no one bothered her.
My love is still sleeping
Covers over his head
So cold it is outside, wished I was in bed.
Another day dawning, crisp, fresh and new
The windows are frosty, a cold morning dew.
Let's go for a walk, wear our hats and our gloves
And embrace this morning with purpose and love.
The things that we're dreaming
And ideas that we share
And listen intently to show that we care
About all that is happening
Right now in our life
With compassion and courage
As husband and wife.

Gratitude

I'm grateful for this morning
A new day has begun
No matter what has happened
What I have or have not done
No matter if the sky is gray
No matter if its blue
I just know that I am grateful
That I can say is true.
I'm grateful for the work I do
And grateful for my home
I'm grateful for my children
And this great earth to roam.
When gratitude is in my heart
God's eternal plan I see
Of giving and receiving
And serving selflessly.

Lunar Celebration

This heaviness is in my head
My thoughts are all mixed up
Am I allowed to speak my piece
Or should I just shut-up
I know the reasons, I believe,
For me, have made me hurt
But he doesn't want to hear it now
He whispers that I'm a jerk
I wonder what he's thinking
I decide to take a ride
Let the wind blow through my hair
And as I travel here and there
I notice soon that I don't care
And now around me everywhere
A peaceful feeling I declare.

I am free to be me.

The moon is full
For all to see
The air is warm a gentle breeze
The sky is big
The stars a glow
And Jupiter is quite a show
Saw four moons all in a row.

Peace of Mind

We can only wonder
How and why and where
Of our life existence
Here on earth we share

What of the life before this
And the one to come
Of birth or death or heartache
Or happiness for some

Answers to these questions
We hear them everyday
But never pay attention
I have one more thing to say

Faith it will move mountains
Seek and ye shall find
Knock the door will open
With these come peace of mind

The Healing

Dimly lit, the stage is bare
Shadows on the wall
A haunting chill, stately and still
A messenger does call
Hear ye hear ye young and fair
Hearken one and all
Gather here, offer your ear
A message for you all.

The vagueness of the shadows
Dark and undefined
Lead you there somewhat aware
Who knows what you will find
Hear ye hear ye people
Hearken to divine
A noble voice
speaks, "it's a choice
For all of humankind
Give yourself permission
And open up your heart
To become whole, reach for your soul
Forgive and love impart
Become aware of what you feel
Choose carefully what you say
For guidance, ASK on any task
You will be shown the way."

The curtain never closes
It's lighter than before
A peaceful tone, you're not alone
Our teachers do implore
Hear ye hear ye brethren
Hearken reverent ones
Release your fears and cry your tears
The Healing has begun.

Understanding

To understand about the world
Would take ten million years
And even then
Would make all men
Shed just as many tears

For understanding everything
Is quite impossible
For only God
And God alone
Is this feat possible

Waiting

These days it seems that waiting
Is what I do the most
For clients or my husband
It slows me to a coast.

I do not mind this waiting
Not even one little bit
Somehow it just seems perfect
It gives me time to sit.

I've been enjoying nature
Butterflies and bees
Sitting by a creek side
Listening to the trees.

I guess that I am thankful
For this waiting game
Reflecting - Being quiet
It helps to keep me sane.

What is real

Our lives are mixed together
By choice we made it so
Loving and committed
Where happiness could grow

Instead of blending harmony
A home where love would stay
We created something
Please make it go away

It's easy to be happy
When you share the same desires
I'm sorry if this scares you
And I've lost the burning fire

You know what? I still love you
And I probably always will
But you have lost the insight
Of knowing what is real.

Whatever Happens

I've learned whatever happens
Happens for the best
No matter who it happens to
Just me or all the rest
Sometimes I am the teacher
Sometimes I'm being taught
And knowing this has helped me
I've realized a lot
Never take for granted
Anyone or anything
Open up your heart and mind
And let your spirit sing
It's okay to be sensitive
It's even good to cry
Listening and learning
And finally knowing why
Share your wisdom wisely
You cannot fail the test
And know whatever happens
Happens for the best.

Miscommunication and Unmet Expectations

Trying to please everyone
Is the surest way to fail
And urge to speak and feeling weak
And yet to no avail.
It's about our expectations
We don't all think the same
A point of view You can't undo
The transmission is to blame.
That's miscommunication
It happens this is true
A shoulder chipped And so tight lipped
From a simple misconstrue.

Some think they're Queen of England
And dismiss you from their sight
You don't exist to this royalist
And nothing makes it right.
Some are Miss Congenial
With their heart out on their sleeve
Their self defend   To comprehend
A perception to perceive.
Is a gift of money
A gift as it would seem?
Choiceless and now voiceless
An underhanded scheme
Does it come with expectations
You know I have a few
I guess I expect we should connect
Even if they don't want to.
Do we take a chance to fix it?
Do we never speak again?
Will it subside or more divide?
Does someone need to win?
The conclusion I have come to
I believe for me is true
Honor one another
There's not much else that you can do.
It only matters in the moment
So do your best each day
Just be aware   And don't despair
Who cares anyway!

Friends/Oneness

The sun will shine
The wind will blow
The stars will gleam
The moon will glow
And when these four they cease to be
You can find them all in me
Because I am here for you my friend
My sun shines on and never ends
My wind will blow your blues away
My stars will gleam
to light your way
My moon will glow and you will be
Happy for Eternity

Blue Moon

Winters sky is calling
Conditions are wide screen
A shade to pull
The moon is full
The night is clear and clean.

Share this moment with me
It's long to come again
Put down the book
And take a look
It's quite a specimen.

Why don't we play Van's Moon Dance
Or Dylan or Greg Brown
Or if you choose
Put on some blues
Then come and settle down.

It's glorious this night sky
It's Big It's Bright It's Bold
The moon is blue
The stars are too
Mesmerizing to behold.

Dark Clouds

What are all these dark clouds
On my sunshine day
Dark and dim and oh so grim
How do I break away?

I have seen the oddness
Like a monster raving mad
Mellow and meek somewhat a freak
A loneliness that's sad

I can hear them crying out
For someone to love
It's not their aim to make it rain
Dark clouds can't see above.

I can feel them yearning
For the big blue sky
Their gloomy shroud a thundercloud
Rendered dissatisfied

I shall not forsake them
But I claim my sunshine days
The wind my voice, it is my choice
To have them on their way.

Summer Thunderstorm

What a way to end the day
Another masterpiece
Just stepped outside to catch a ride
And wait for rain to cease.
Like a monsoon coming down
Water rushing by
Hard to explain the mercury rain
Glistening in my eye.
Clouds shadow all the parking lot
Sun on the school next door
In front of me a giant tree,
And this I've never seen before
A double rainbow end to end

The colors magnified
In a daze   So much to gaze
And me so open-eyed
With everything around me
A friend to share the scene
Extraordinaire   Beyond compare
It washed the city clean
The spectacle continues
As evening passes through
And shapes unfold   In clouds of gold
Like cottonballs into
Many little cherub babes
Slowly moving east
And in the west   The color best
For ones eyes to feast
A color -   For the artist
A challenge to display
A turquoise blue   So bright and true
What a way to end the day.

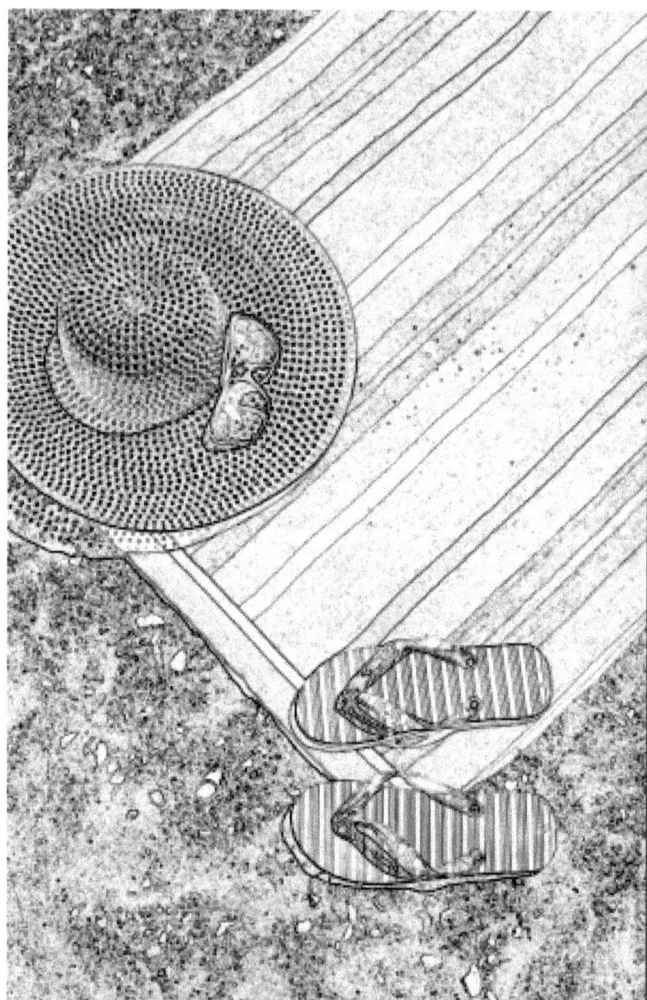

Summertime Blues

Today is hot and sweltering
One hundred one degrees
The bugs are thick
My skin did stick
To the seat in Tommy's jeep.

Too tired to go walking
Too tired to play at all
To beat the heat
I put my feet
In the fountain at the mall.

I'm cranky and I'm sweating
My lemonade is hot
All I foresee is misery
A genuine fuss-pot.

Sunshine Fall Day

Cool the breeze with gentle ease
Sky cloudless clear and blue
Bask in the sun
A nap sounds fun
All afternoon with you
The perfect way to spend the day
In lazy autumn time
No one to please
Just you to squeeze
My favorite pastime.

The Swing

There is a little hilltop park
Up in my neighborhood
Where I can walk and balance rock
It makes me feel so good.
But what I have my sights on
Before I leave the house
The special thing, that is the swing
And yes there is no doubt.
I pretend like I am flying
Free from all my cares
Ever soaring and exploring
Few things can compare.
Yes, I like swings in daytime
And especially at night
I'll give up swings
When I grow wings
'Till then they are my flight.

Kings Row

The coaches and carriages are now buses and cars
The castles are mansions you see from afar
The people are different and yet they're the same
Coming and going not knowing their names

Some in a hurry, some putzing by
Some hanging out laundry looking up at the sky
Some are on bicycles, skateboards and blades
Some are out walking looking for shade

The folks all around here I know only a few
Unlike the old days all our neighbors we knew
Some say it was easier, a time one could rest
Less struggle and heartache when life was the best

I say NOW is important it's always the same
Time softens the memory and takes away pain
We can't help but move forward and leave past behind
We're still on the journey to better mankind

So here on the hilltop with a garden below
I'll choose to be happy in Kingdom Kings Row.

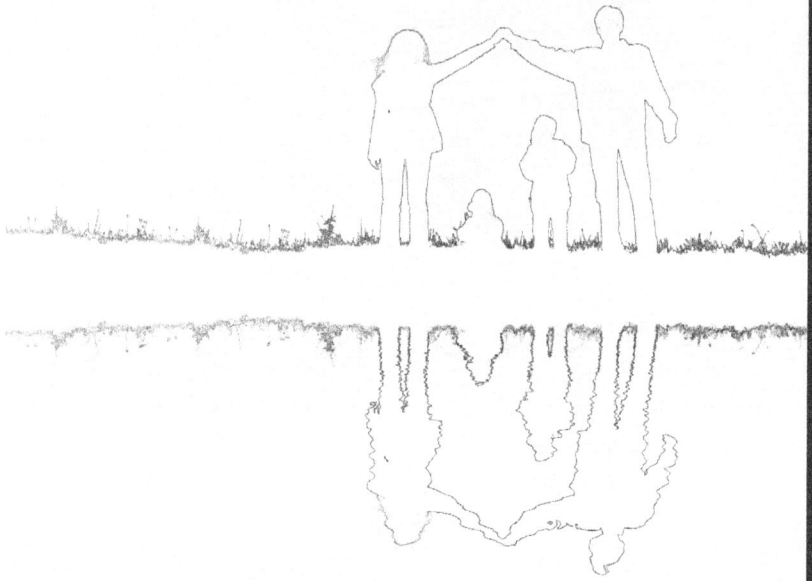

Kings Beach

Mother and Child dancing
Seagull eating trash
Cell phone ringing
Children singing
Swimmers kick and splash
Windy waves are crashing
On the sandy shore
Lovers kiss
A Frisbee miss
The slam of a car door
Pine trees all above me
Majestic mountains high
Screeching heard
A baby bird
A noisy boat goes by
There's solitude within me
And people all around
Another day
I'll be okay
With my feet back on the ground

Burning Man 1999

A curious village develops
As artists and builders move in
With wood, lights and wire
And more than desire
Let the man-making begin.
Over 22,000 expected
The flow of a new tribe arrive
With creative inventions
And peaceful intentions
Bring a once a year city alive.
Organized and user friendly
An address for everyone
Wisely divided

With a portion provided
For those who need rest from the fun.
There are so many things to consider
Like safety, sanitation and such.
There's been growing pain
And permits to obtain
Legalities most wouldn't touch
The Medic the Ranger the Sheriff
Are a big part of the scene
The warning is stated
And re-indicated
The risk and the danger foreseen.
But it only gets better and better
As art cars and people appear.
Come late afternoon
All the players in tune
A musical dust atmosphere.
There is everything you can imagine
And there's no money to spend
A gift and bartering place
When you leave, "LEAVE NO TRACE"
No wonder so many attend.
NEON, the fashion for night time
Whatever glows in the dark
Costume or no clothes
And yes, anything goes.
It's fireworks, flames and great art.
The lasers they get you excited
As they raise up and light up 'the Man'.

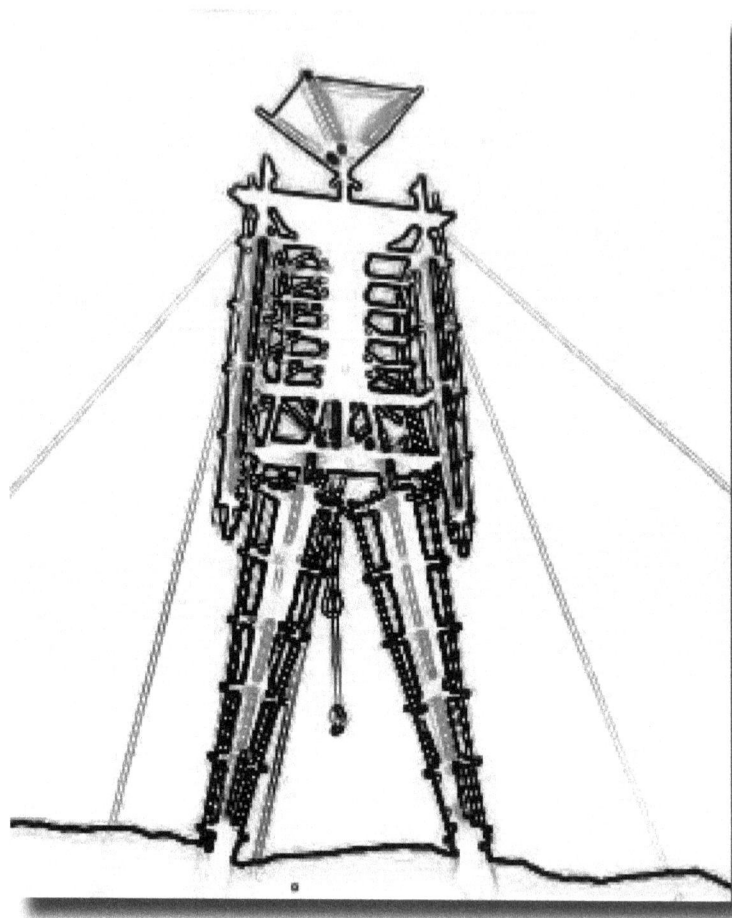

As the crowd energizes
The volume it rises,
The Burning is so close at hand.
Some of them like front and center
For me, I stay some distance back
I like a view
That included the crowd too,
Safe from unknowing attack.
The dancing and drumming continue
The milky way brighter than bright
The playa vibrating
The sound penetrating
Till morning past dawns early light.
Somehow this is rejuvenating
A happening so fabulous
Some left right away
Some chose to delay
And join in the mass exodus
This is my wish for the future
Not knowing what 'this' may become
Let the Golden Rule
Be totally cool
In the next millennium.

Jamie girl

Since you were only two weeks old
I have memorized your face
You fit right in with Chris and Kim
That no one can replace.
You're witty and your charming
And turning 21
The likelihood of womanhood
Has more than just begun.
Your accomplishments are many
You're busy as a bee
You play out late
And steady date
Your GQ man JC.
You have compassion for your loved ones
No tolerance for a fool.
Fast talking girl
And what a pearl
A 3.5 at school.
I'm sure you know I love you
Just like you were my own
Invent your tune
Reach for the moon
At this life milestone.

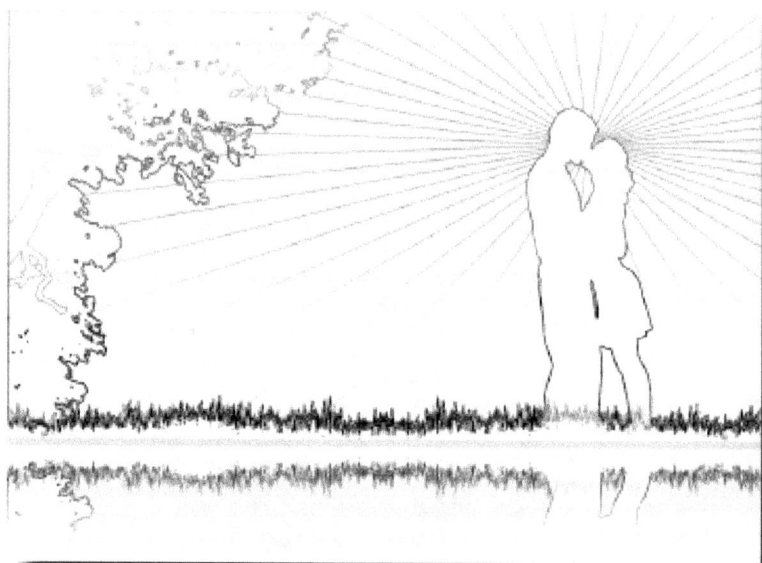

Kimberlee Michele
On your 20th birthday

My darling girl I love you so
You've grown before my eyes
You are lovely and you're graceful
I hope you realize
Life has so much in store for you
It's only just begun
Be willing and be open
Let yourself be number one.
There are so many seasons
In this journey we call life
Some are very difficult
Full of woe and strife.
Some look like they will never end
Somehow they always do
And we're always better for it
Stronger and wiser too.
As we look back and joy and sorrow
The good times and the bad
It gives us some perspective
Grateful that we have
The knowledge that will get us through
Seasons that are hard
Remembering that, It shall pass
And you'll be dealt another card.

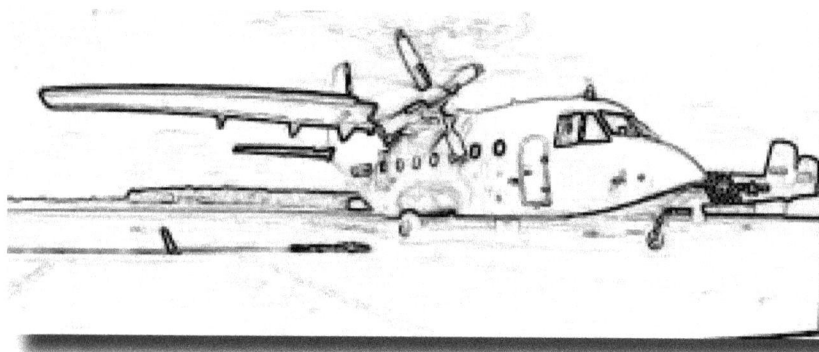

Farewell

It's getting closer to the day
That we shall say farewell
A journey starts in young men's hearts
And in their soul does dwell.
To leave his home and family
Independence to declare
Learn a trade   Become self made
And ever more aware
Good-bye dear son we love you
More than you'll ever know
The world you'll see, we guarantee
You cannot help but grow
Another door has opened
An adventure to begin
Seek the truth   Not just in youth
Understand self-discipline
Bear in mind that passion
For everything you do
Is what it takes to make or break
And always see you through
We'll see you in the future
The man you have become
What you employ to bring you joy
To the beat of your own drum.

Own This Moment...
OWN
WON
NOW

OWN

Three letters
Three words
OWN
WON
NOW

NOW is such a simple word
To the point
And short
Now not then
And now not when
This moment don't distort

Backwards you have WON the prize
A gift we call the present
Know now is here
Though when is near
And then has surely been spent

OWN is yet another way
Let your spirit show you how
Release debris
And be set free
Live in the here and now.

About the author

Deborah Baptiste Lee was born in Chula Vista,
California, April 3, 1956. She makes her home
in Reno, Nevada where she enjoys her family and
friends and continues to be inspired by everyday life.

Join Deborah at her blog for updates, news and
discussions at Dragonflyblog.com

www.ingramcontent.com/pod-product-compliance
Lightning Source LLC
Chambersburg PA
CBHW060051050426
42448CB00011B/2398